BE FRUITFUL AND MULTIPLY

Why Economics Is Necessary for Making God-Pleasing Decisions

Anne Bradley

INSTITUTE FOR
FAITH, WORK
& ECONOMICS

First Edition, 2016
ISBN 978-0-9975369-0-4

Published by the
Institute for Faith, Work & Economics
8400 Westpark Drive
Suite 100
McLean, Virginia 22102

www.tifwe.org

BE FRUITFUL AND MULTIPLY

Why Economics Is Necessary for Making God-Pleasing Decisions

CONTENTS

INTRODUCTION

Have you ever lost sleep at night because you were worried about the performance of Gross Domestic Product (GDP) last quarter? Have you ever prayed specifically about GDP? Most of us do not worry about these things because they seem remote, distant, academic, and inapplicable to our daily lives.

Have you ever prayed for people that are starving and oppressed at the hands of dictators? I bet you have and do. The difference is that one seems to matter and the other seems like ivory-tower textbook dribble. The blame lies with economists, not you. What if I told you that economics is code for making prudent decisions in all areas of life? That seems like something we can all get on board with, something that we should commit to prayer, and something deserving of great attention.

I want to make the radical claim that if we ignore the economic way of thinking as part of making God-honoring decisions, many lives will be at stake. Not only will we suffer personally, but ignoring economic principles will shatter lives on a societal level.

It is argued that nearly 20 million people lost their lives under the communist regime in the Soviet Union during the twentieth century. In the famous book *The Black Book of Communism*, editor Stéphane Courtois claims that communist regimes turned mass crimes into a "full-blown system of government." If you look at the death tolls from communism across countries, the death toll becomes a staggering 94 million. Some scholars estimate that the number is much higher.[1]

We are all image-bearers of God, and each of us has tremendous dignity and worth. Economic systems should enable us to use our gifts, encourage us to serve others, and allow us to flourish, not destroy us. Scripture and sound economic thinking can protect us from these atrocities, but only if we adhere to principles of truth that will lead us to greater flourishing rather than mass executions and starvation. As it is written in II Timothy 3:16-17, "All Scripture is God-breathed and is useful for teaching, rebuking, correcting and training in righteousness, so that the servant of God may be thoroughly equipped for every good work." We know that principles found in Scripture are given to us by God for our benefit.

When societies allow people the freedom to pursue God's will for their lives, God is glorified and flourishing increases. When societies deny their citizens the freedom to pursue their God-given callings, suffering, poverty, hopelessness, despair, and oppression result. As the twentieth century episodes with communism and central planning demonstrate, lives are destroyed when we don't adhere to God's design for us and his desires for his creation.

I witnessed these horrible outcomes firsthand when I was a teenager. I took a school trip to the former Soviet Union before its official economic collapse in 1991. I had no formal or proper understanding of economics at the time, but my exposure to life under communism kick-started my journey to becoming an economist and my desire to understand what I witnessed.

When we arrived in Moscow, we were greeted by an official Soviet liaison who was by our side the entire trip. As we toured Moscow, we were forbidden from seeing the destitute life of subsistence farming in the rural regions. Although the Soviets were desperately trying to paint a picture of flourishing, it wasn't hard to see through the ruse. The beautiful Kremlin and colorful domes of St. Basil's Cathedral were veneers attempting to hide the godless culture and gray desperation that enveloped everyone.

When a government takes over all economic activity, there are drastic consequences that affect all of life and society. I witnessed those. Controlling all economic activity requires a strong dictatorship and totalitarian measures of oppression and violence. The society requires individuals to divorce themselves from who God created them to be and serve the state instead. With this comes state-sponsored atheism, which is an effort to control culture and destroy individual identities.

While my trip was an invaluable, eye-opening experience, I had never been so happy to return home to a place where I was free in so many fundamental ways. The US granted me freedom to worship Jesus and follow his direction for my life, and the freedom to make decisions that promote flourishing. These freedoms were absent in the former Soviet Union. I left there with important questions:

- Why was I born into a free society and afforded things that some people could only dream of?

- Was there a way to fix what I saw?

- How does a country that had suffered under the violent massacre of state-imposed central planning emerge from the dark into greater freedom?

What I now understand is that the Soviet Union failed for the same reasons that Venezuela and North Korea are failing today. The government of Venezuela is losing its grip of their futile efforts to control the economic choices of individuals. Suffering and oppression are the result. North Korea is desperately poor, while South Korea has a thriving economy. They share similar ethnic backgrounds and conditions of geography, but one is thriving while the other is suffering because its society is not organized in the way that God designed it.

Cultures and countries fail when leaders construct a society that operates opposite of God's design. If we want to protect the innocent citizens that are harmed in these environments, we must understand the framework for flourishing that God gives us in Scripture. We are created in his image with a specific purpose for this particular time and place. When we fulfill his purposes, we glorify him. When we revolt against them, whether of our own accord or through government oppression, we suffer the consequences.

The Soviet Union was a terrible failure because it revolted against God's design and desire for his creation. We are created in God's image and commanded to do important things with our gifts and talents, mainly to serve others, which glorifies God. The economic system of the Soviet Union failed because it denied people the ability to live into who God created them to be. It stripped citizens of their personal choices and provided no incentives for people to unleash their creativity in productive ways. The economy was unproductive because individuals were not encouraged to be productive. Instead, citizens were treated as cogs in the machinery of the state, only existing for its purposes. For example, in societies where people are encouraged to be creative through economic exchange, one can walk into a grocery store and choose from dozens of loaves of bread. The Soviet system stamped out the engine of human creativity. As a result, bread was scarce, a corrupt black market for basics food items emerged, and many starved.

These macroeconomic systems failed because they were a revolt against our design and our human nature. A society that is built on sand cannot stand forever. It is why nations like North Korea live in poverty and fear today. Societies must be built on the firm foundation of human creativity and limited abilities, which requires that we are able to engage in economic exchange and trade. When we recognize both our abilities and limitations, systems naturally develop that allow us to rely on each other. The problem with North Korea and the Soviet Union is that there were no grocers, butchers, and other entrepreneurs on whom people could rely.

To understand the requirements for a flourishing society, we must begin with an understanding of who we are as humans and what we are here to accomplish. Without understanding God's desires, we cannot make decisions that please him. Without understanding how he created us, we cannot grasp our limits and capabilities.

It might be tempting to look at the Soviet Union as an extreme case. Surely, what happened there cannot happen again. The terrifying reality is that if citizens lose enough of their freedoms and their ability to serve God and contribute to the flourishing of his creation, history can and will repeat itself. The current conditions in Venezuela demonstrate this truth. Grocery stores are empty and bank accounts have dwindled, making ordinary life and what used to be ordinary tasks, like shopping for bread, impossible.

To flourish on a societal level, each of us must be able to do what God has made us to do. We must be able to wake up in the morning to cultivate our talents and pursue our desires. The heart of human flourishing comes from the knowledge that we are made in the image of God, that we are here for a reason, and that every decision of our lives matters–big and small. We can take nothing for granted and all of our decisions, from what we eat for breakfast to whom we marry, matter. These decisions can both honor and glorify God, or they can defy God's desires and bring greater suffering. When we live in a society where we are able and encouraged to be productive with our talents, we benefit not just ourselves but others, and in this, we honor God. When we restrict that freedom, both individuals and society suffer because we are forced to do many things on our own.

Economics is essential to pleasing God because it is about making personal choices under conditions of scarcity. As part of our human condition, we are constantly making decisions. In this regard, you are already an economist! You weigh the expected costs against the expected benefits of your choices, and you do this because you naturally seek profit. If you decrease your commute to work, you profit by gaining time. The profit of time allows you to steward more of your energy in productive arenas that depend upon your gifts. The assertion of this book is that we are called to be profit-maximizers, which is the goal of stewardship. We have limited time, limited talent, and limited treasure. We are asked to use these gifts with their limitations to the fullest, and when we do that well, we have more leftovers (profit). The more time, talent, and treasure that is left over, the more we can serve others and fulfill God's desires for us.

This booklet will start in Genesis, where we can understand God's design and answer the question, "How did we get here?" This in turn helps us fulfill his desires for his creation. A proper understanding of our "marching orders" presented in the beginning of Scripture reveals that stewardship is our main job. Stewardship is the process, or the means, we employ for utilizing all we are and all we have to further God's kingdom.

Next, we will explore why we are here to truly understand our unique purpose on earth. Then we will examine the basic realities of economic thinking given to us in Scripture that help us navigate our lives to the glory of God. Biblical economic institutions like property rights, the rule of law, and freedom, allow us the proper operating environment to fulfill the role that God gives each of us. When we are able to fulfill this role, we experience and contribute to greater societal flourishing.

Certain measures help us evaluate if we are doing this effectively on a societal level. The *Index of Economic Freedom* is a helpful tool to measure societal flourishing and develop the most productive operating environment for effective stewardship. A society with higher levels of economic freedom affords ordinary citizens, like you and me, the opportunity to live how God has called us to live. My visit to the former Soviet Union was a stark picture of what happens when people try to operate in an environment without economic freedom – great suffering and death.

The former Soviet Union was plagued with material shortages and spiritual bankruptcy, which bred despair and hopelessness. It provided a painfully accurate picture of the societal consequences of individual limitations to freely stewarding God's resources. When people are not free to do what God has called them to do, they perish. However, the gospel gives great hope for the world. This booklet will unpack complex concepts of freedom, economics, decision-making, and flourishing while also providing practical steps for becoming better stewards. If we don't steward our time, talent, and treasure well, we are forcing others to suffer because we are not serving them as well as we could.

CHAPTER 1: **HOW DID WE GET HERE?**

Tugging at the hearts of men and women around the world are deep-seated questions of purpose and fulfillment. *Why am I here? What is my purpose? Does the minutiae of my life matter?*

The only way to answer these questions is to start at the beginning of Scripture. To know *why* we are here, we must first explore *how* we got here.

The creation account detailed in Genesis gives us the divine context for our existence. We are not here by chance. We are formed by the creative imagination and hand of God, made in his image and likeness (Gen. 1:25-28). We are here precisely because God put us here. This reality instills great dignity, purpose, and immeasurable value within us. Genesis 1:25-28 informs us both about the nature of God and the nature of mankind:

> God made the wild animals according to their kinds, the livestock according to their kinds, and all the creatures that move along the ground according to their kinds. And God saw that it was good. Then God said, "Let us make mankind in our image, in our likeness, so that they may rule over the fish in the sea and the birds in the sky, over the livestock and all the wild animals, and over all the creatures that move along the ground." So God created mankind in his own image, in the image of God he created them; male and female he created them. God blessed them and said to them, "Be fruitful and increase in number; fill the earth and subdue it. Rule over the fish in the sea and the birds in the sky and over every living creature that moves on the ground."

What does it mean to be created in God's image? In *Systematic Theology,* Wayne Grudem points out that the words used in Genesis 1:26-27, "image" (tselem) and "likeness" (demut), in the Hebrew "refer to something that is similar but not identical to the thing that it represents or is the 'image' of." Genesis 1:26 "would have meant to the original readers, 'Let us make man to be like us and to represent us.'"[2] The Hebrew root of the Latin phrase for image of God–*imago Dei*–means image, shadow, or likeness of God. You are a snapshot or facsimile of God. At the very least, this means humans occupy a higher place in the created order because we alone are imprinted with god-like characteristics. Even more so, imaging God is a central aspect of our fundamental created order. To be fully human is to reflect God's creative, spiritual, intelligent, communicative, relational, moral, and purposeful characteristics.[3] By realizing our gifts to their utmost potential, we are most obedient to God's design.

Human existence is a special, authoritative indicator of the creative power of God. God created man out of nothing (*ex nihilo*). He is a maker, an author, a creator, and a worker. We harbor an aspect of this creative ability in our capability to create something out of what God has already given us. Only God can create something out of nothing, but by forming us in his image, we can create value from and improve upon his creation. We are commanded to do nothing less.

Not only do we reflect God's characteristics, but as his image-bearers, we have specific duties to fill. We are the only creatures commanded to fill the earth and subdue it, and to have dominion over all of creation (Gen. 1:28). We roam the earth with all of God's creatures, but we also *rule* the earth and God's creatures. God created us with the capability and the responsibility to reign over his earthly creation.

Understanding the implications of being made in the image of God is the first step toward living into full appreciation of who we are and what we are made to do. Fully appreciating the context of our creation helps foster great personal fulfillment because it brings awareness to God's intentional design of and desires for his creation. You will find great pleasure and fulfillment when who God made you to be and what he has called you to do are fully developed and expressed.

Being made in the image and likeness of God means we are unique, we have purpose, and we are limited. Scientists have studied snowflakes and have found that no two snowflakes are exactly alike. This analogy helps us understand our intricate, non-replicable, intentional design. Just as God fashions each snowflake uniquely, he has made you specifically different from everyone else. Your complex strand of DNA makes you distinct from every single human being to ever walk the earth. Just think – we are far more valued and precious than snowflakes, flowers, and all other elements of God's creation (Matt. 6:26)!

It is God's intentional design for no two humans to be the same. Our distinct uniqueness points to God's infinite power and gives us purpose. Humans are the crowning splendor of God's hand (Is. 62:3). Not only does God create us all differently, but he also gives each person a specific purpose. Each of us is his unique workmanship for the role he designed specifically for us to play (Eph. 2:10). The role we have in the kingdom of God is one that no one else can occupy. Each role in the kingdom is vital. There is no role that is more important than another because God has woven all things together for his purposes—just like the intricate working of the human body. Paul explains this in I Corinthians 12:5-7:

> There are different kinds of gifts, but the same Spirit distributes them. There are different kinds of service, but the same Lord. There are different kinds of working, but in all of them and in everyone it is the same God at work. Now to each one the manifestation of the Spirit is given for the common good.

We are made in the image of God, but we are not God so we face limitations. This was true before the fall of man. We each have twenty-four hours in a day and limited means and knowledge to accomplish everything we desire. This was true before our sin, and it is true and exacerbated after our sin. Adam and Eve had to tinker and learn and think and develop skills. They were finite just as we are. What they had that we do not is an infinite time horizon. The costs of learning and tinkering are lower when you have forever to figure something out. For us, the story is not the same. If we don't find newer and better ways of doing things, a lot more is at stake.

Our limitations are the reason we need to come together through economic exchange. If I can trade some of my income for heart surgery, I am decidedly better off than if I am left to do heart surgery on my own. In fact, I will surely perish if I must rely on myself. This is true of heart surgery and growing bananas. If I have to figure out how to produce all the things I need and desire, I am left with little and so are others. However, if I am blessed with the space to learn who I am in God and develop my skills, I can improve my skills and serve others with them. It frees me from having to figure out how to do everything and allows me more options. I can choose from bananas, apples, and strawberries at the grocery store. If I were left to my own devices, I would likely have none of those options.

We are here because God designed us with distinct and unique gifts to cultivate his creation. We are here because he put us here to serve him and bring him glory. We can only do this within a community. That community is brought together through exchange and allows us to fulfill God's desires for his creation.

CHAPTER 2: **WHY ARE WE HERE?**
The Four-Chapter Gospel

K nowing how we got here is only half the battle; the pressing question on the heart of every person is to understand their significance in this world. *What can I possibly do that matters? I'm just an accountant; I'm not saving lives. What is my purpose?* Have you ever stared blankly into the computer screen at the email you are constructing and wondered what difference it could possibly make? I know I have.

These are the universal longings of our souls. We have a universal desire to matter and to offer something special to the world. The first chapter of the Bible helps us understand that our dignity comes from our creation in God. Scripture gives us answers about why we are here, and it gives us renewed purpose to go into the world and do it well. To understand God's greater purposes for his people and how we fit into it, we must explore what some call the meta-story of the Bible, also known as the four-chapter gospel.

The four-chapter gospel is not a new or different gospel from the biblical story presented in Scripture. What most Christians understand can be explained by 1) our sin and 2) our need for a savior, found in Jesus Christ. These truths are universally true for all humankind. But the gospel of Jesus Christ is about more than sin and salvation; it encompasses God's grand purpose for his entire creation, from the first verse of Genesis to the last verse in Revelation. The four-chapter gospel captures the greatest story ever told, a love story of significance from God to his people. The four chapters help explain the grand narrative that is present throughout every page of Scripture. Within this gospel, you have a specific role.

The four chapters of the gospel are Creation, Fall, Redemption, Restoration. The chapter of Creation explains the way things were in the very beginning. The Fall explains the way things are because of Adam's original sin and its effects on the whole of creation. The chapter of Redemption shows the way things could be because of the work of Christ on our behalf. Finally, the chapter of Restoration reveals the way things will be at the end of this age. This is the ultimate story of purpose and significance.

The first chapter of Creation pictures the glory of God's perfect creation (Gen. 1:31). We learn about God's nature, that he is a worker, an artist, and a maker. He created the world in perfect harmony and flourishing, and he was pleased. Humankind was the crowning glory of his creation, tasked to care for and cultivate the earth. The whole of creation was "very good" and operated as God intended it—the way things were supposed to be.

In the Fall, we see the whole creation marred by the human mutiny; every part of creation was plunged into the chaos of sin (Rom. 8:19-20). Adam and Eve's rebellion against God unleashed sin upon the world and forever separated humankind from the presence of God. Sin tainted all humankind's relationships with God, others, and creation.

In the third chapter of Redemption we see the beginning of the restoration and fulfillment of God's original purposes through the work of Jesus Christ (Heb. 9:11-14). Because of God's love for his people, he paid the eternal price for sin – death – so that his people may be restored to a right relationship with him. He sent his only son to die for the sins of all his people, past, present, and future. While the brokenness of the world is still very apparent in this third chapter, the hope of the restoration of all things is secured through the work of Christ and clearly demonstrated through the witness of his followers.

In the final chapter, Restoration, Christ will complete the work he started and will make all things new. Scripture tells us that "there shall be no more death, nor sorrow, nor crying. There shall be no more pain, for the former things [will] have passed away" (Rev. 21:4). The biblical picture of restoration is a new city on the new earth (Rev. 21:1-2). It is a symbol of human progress that gives us hope for our work here on earth. Restoration is the completion of God's purposes for his creation so that he may walk with his people and be glorified for all eternity.

This is the comprehensive gospel story that explains why we are here and where we are going.

When we see the Bible through the perspective of these four chapters, from beginning to end, we better understand who we are, why we are here, and how it matters.

Understanding this larger story is critical for knowing how precious we are in God's sight and the importance of doing our jobs well. God did not have to include us in his redemptive mission, but because of his love for us, he requires us to help further his kingdom until Christ returns. We can only experience true joy when we do what God has ultimately designed us to do. This also brings great significance to our lives. God did not create us to run around engaging in useless, time-consuming activities to await his return. Instead, he created us to use our gifts to serve his creation, bring him glory, and contribute to greater human flourishing. In doing this, we help bring about a state of affairs that is closer or more aligned with the way things were supposed to be as we anticipate his return.

We are here to glorify God because he created all of creation for his own glory. We glorify God when we do what he created us to do in the way he wants us to do it. He created you specially to do something. It does not matter whether you are a pastor, a janitor, or a CEO. You are the only you there ever was or ever has been. Doing your best means figuring out your purpose given to you by God and pursuing it well.

The four-chapter gospel is the answer to age-old questions of significance. It tells us why we are here. We see this idea in the opening chapter of Genesis when we read about the six days of creation. At the end of each of the first five days, God looks at his creation and declares that it is good (Gen 1:12, 18, 21, 25). At the end of the sixth day, "God saw all that he had made, and it was *very* good" (Gen. 1:31, emphasis mine). God was delighted with all of his work and when he looked at it, it pleased him and brought him joy. God saw it not just as "good" but as "very good." *Very* is an adverb meaning "extremely", "exceedingly", or "in a high degree."[4] God's creation is as good as possible because it reflects him in all of his glory. Here we find the first hint of God's original intent for his creation. The purpose of God is to find pleasure and be glorified by his creation (Ps. 19; Rev. 4:11). He looks out on the creation and sees everything that he has made is working together just as he planned.

Integrated into creation is a great truth of the created universe that is often overlooked. The word that best describes God's creation is *interdependence.* From the very beginning, a distinct connectedness has tied all of creation together. Before sin entered the world, everything worked together in perfect harmony. Today, we still witness the interconnectedness of creation, even though it is fraught with the frustration of sin. Even in spite of our sin, we know that God is working all things together for good for those that love him and have been called according to his purpose (Rom. 8:28-30). We are here to fulfill God's purposes, which he has pre-determined from before the beginning of time.

We are made for community. We need each other because we are not God; we are not omnipotent and cannot do all things perfectly. Moreover, when we try to complete tasks beyond our abilities, we find ourselves frustrated by our own futility and left without the very things we need. God's perfect design of interdependence is for our own benefit because left on our own, we would not thrive. We cannot live alone.

Our finite, limited design requires us to rely on each other and brings us into trading relationships, reinforcing the relational aspect of God that we reflect. This happens on a very basic level in our homes. One person may be better at paying the bills while the other is better at grocery shopping. It behooves husbands, wives, and children to understand this just as it benefits churches, jobs, and society to implement this. When we can exchange based on our strengths, we can profit more. When we can profit more, we can serve others more and honor God.

Understanding the larger story of Scripture and our role in it helps us better understand our purpose: to glorify God and to bring about greater flourishing and *shalom*, the Old Testament concept of universal peace that we will explore in chapter four.

CHAPTER 3: **WHY ARE WE HERE?**
Understanding Our Purpose

Genesis helps us understand how we got here and why it matters, giving us context for life on earth. God created the world and each one of us in a specific way to glorify him. Our job is to pursue a life that honors God's design and fulfills his calling for our lives and his creation. If we look at the narrative of Genesis, it is one of abundance. The rivers are teaming with fish, birds fill the skies, and every tree-bearing fruit on the entire earth is given to man, except for one. Out of darkness and nothing, God created abundance. This helps us understand God's desires for his creation – richness and abundance.

On the sixth day of creation, when God declared it "very good", all the necessary elements were present to work together for his purposes. The flowers require sunlight. The bees require flowers for their pollen. The lizards eat the bees. Bears and humans eat the honey produced by the bees. There is an explicit, observable, and intentional way that all these things work together, yet they are not strictly pragmatic.

They function as a whole operating in harmony, beauty, grandeur, and abundance. When these things work the way they are intended to, they point back to God and glorify him, and there is *shalom.* Shalom is a word that is often translated as "peace" or the absence of conflict, but it has a much richer meaning. Shalom means universal flourishing, wholeness, and delight. It is the way things ought to be. The Old Testament prophets pictured shalom as the wolf living with the lamb, weapons turned into farming tools, deserts blooming, and the mountains streaming with red wine (Is. 2:4, 11:6; Ez. 36:35; Amos 9:13).

Each element of creation has an interconnection with all of the other elements. Humans reflect something different about God's creation. We can reason, think, and decide between many alternatives. We do not strictly operate out of instinct as bees and lizards do. We are here to do much more.

In Genesis 1:28-29, God helps us understand what he wants us to do:

> God blessed them and said to them, "Be fruitful and increase in number; fill the earth and subdue it. Rule over the fish in the sea and the birds in the sky and over every living creature that moves on the ground." Then God said, "I give you every seed-bearing plant on the face of the whole earth and every tree that has fruit with seed in it. They will be yours for food. And to all the beasts of the earth and all the birds in the sky and all the creatures that move along the ground—everything that has the breath of life in it—I give every green plant for food." And it was so.

God would not give us the garden and tell us to cultivate it without giving us the tools we need. In Genesis 2, God continues by giving us our marching orders and our job description. Humans have a special role in the cultivating of God's very good creation. We learn more about this in Genesis 2:15:

> The Lord God took the man and put him in the Garden of Eden to work it and take care of it.

This is our job description as thinking and reasoning human beings made in God's image. We are to do two fundamental things: work his garden and take care of it. To take care of something requires putting work into it and protecting it from destruction. If God asked us just to take care of his garden, we would not alter it. One could imagine that we would stand watch and make sure it remains as is; we would preserve it. In caring for the garden, we might prune it, but we would not be "working it" in the way God asks us.

The word "work" in Hebrew as used in Genesis 2:15 is the verb *abad*, which means "to work or to serve."[5] God explicitly asks us to work his creation and serve him. He tells us to "be fruitful and increase in number; fill the earth and subdue it" (Gen. 1:28). God desires us to multiply, prosper, cultivate, and enjoy his good creation. This is our ultimate purpose, also known as the cultural mandate. To prepare us for this noble task, God has given us all the tools and raw materials necessary to do our job well. God's intentional design of man fits perfectly with his design for all of creation. God does not hold us to impossible expectations; he equips us to accomplish this task with the tools he has given us.

Ephesians 2:10 reinforces the message given to us first in Genesis:

> For we are God's handiwork, created in Christ Jesus to do good works, which God prepared in advance for us to do.

Before the onset of time, God knew his plan and desires for creation. Creation would work together to bring him glory and honor. We are his special, unique, and diverse handiwork, and he has prepared us in advance to do the things today that allow us to be part of advancing his creation toward greater human flourishing.

Recall that the word "abad" means to serve. We are here to use our gifts and our time to cultivate God's creation and to serve others, and we do this best when we do what God put us here to do and rely on his intended interdependence. We are able to leave the planet with more flourishing than was here before we were born. What an awesome responsibility that we have the privilege of undertaking! When we serve God and his creation, God is glorified.

Our job is to unleash our human creativity on the planet until Christ returns. While Ephesians 2:10 helps us to understand what we are made to do – good works. Colossians 1:10 emphasizes how we know when we are doing good works.

> So that you may live a life worthy of the Lord and please him in every way: bearing fruit in every good work, growing in the knowledge of God.

We are worthy as stewards when we bear fruit in every good work, and this is what pleases God. Making God-pleasing decisions means we must learn what he created us to do, please him in every way, and bear fruit in every good work. This applies to the large decisions and the small, the monumental choices and the minutiae of our lives.

While understanding our job description helps us accomplish God's purpose, our sin makes this difficult. The reason for this difficulty, which always brings despair and frustration, is because our sin is a revolt against God's economy and his intended means by which we should operate. God calls us back to his original purposes, but our sin makes us resist. We desire complete independence, control, and power, but that runs counter to God's design. If we want to please God, we must serve him well. When we choose to live apart from him, we face frustration and difficulties. We must fulfill the master's original purpose – shalom. The Fall and our sin make our efforts to please God more difficult, but our job remains.

Despite our sin, we can do the job to which God has graciously called us because of the redemption provided by Jesus. When we do, we both contribute to and experience greater shalom, or flourishing. This is where economics plays an integral role into our effective stewardship of God's creation. When we embrace the economic way of thinking, we are better poised to please God in all that we do, honor him, and bring glory to him and his creation through increased human flourishing. To do that we must realize that life is all about God, not all about us.

CHAPTER 4:
WHAT ARE WE WORKING TOWARD?
Shalom and Flourishing

W hat outcomes are we working toward? How do we know we are successful?

With all the diversity across the human race over thousands of years, one might not expect to find many unifying ideas. Remarkably, there seems to be one meta-concept that transcends all worldviews. Jonathan Pennington writes:

> This concept has staying power and universal voice because it addresses what is most basic and innate to all of humanity, despite the diversity of race, culture, and values. It is a concept that proves to be the motivating force and end goal of all that humans do and think. This idea or theme can be identified as human flourishing… Human flourishing alone is the idea that encompasses all human activity and goals because there is nothing so natural and inescapable as the desire to live, and to live in peace, security, love, health, and happiness. These are not merely cultural values or the desire of a certain people or time period. The desire for human flourishing motivates everything humans do… All human behavior, when analyzed deeply enough, will be found to be motivated by the desire for life and flourishing, individually and corporately. [6]

While no two humans are the same, all hearts have the same intrinsic desire. We are all created in the image of God with the desire to know him, to flourish, whether we acknowledge this or not. It is a universal truth that has been written on our hearts. It is part of our nature and our design, and as such it transcends trends and culture. Ecclesiastes 3:11 says:

He has made everything beautiful in its time. He has also set eternity in the human heart; yet no one can fathom what God has done from beginning to end.

The desire to flourish is written deep within our souls.

This idea of human flourishing is the Old Testament Hebrew concept of *shalom* mentioned previously. Cornelius Plantinga in his book, *Not the Way It's Supposed to Be*, defines shalom as:

> The webbing together of God, humans, and all creation in justice, fulfillment, and delight... Shalom means universal flourishing, wholeness and delight – a rich state of affairs in which natural needs are satisfied and natural gifts fruitfully employed, Shalom, in other words, is the way things ought to be... the full flourishing of human life in all aspects, as God intended it to be.[7]

One of the titles we see in the Old Testament for Christ is the Prince of Peace, but what the passage really says in the Hebrew is that Jesus is the Prince of Shalom (Is. 9:6). Jesus is not just a prince that will come back and stop all the fighting; he is the prince who will come back and restore universal flourishing. His work as the Prince of Shalom "means complete reconciliation, a state of the fullest flourishing in every dimension–physical, emotional, social and spiritual."[8] The redemption brought by Christ is about restoring everything to the way it should be. Shalom bookends human existence. It characterizes the Garden of Eden (the way it was supposed to be) and the eternal City, the New Jerusalem (the way it is going to be), and so provides the vision for our existence in between.[9]

The word shalom is used approximately 250 times in the Hebrew Bible, with the majority of uses describing biblical flourishing. For example, shalom is the climax of the Aaronic or priestly benediction in Numbers 6:24-26, looking forward to the ultimate blessing from God:

The Lord bless you and keep you;

The Lord make his face to shine upon you, and be gracious to you;

The Lord lift up his countenance upon you, and give you **shalom**.
(emphasis added)

The work that God designed for us to do before the onset of time brings about greater levels of flourishing by advancing creation toward shalom, the way things were supposed to be. This happens despite our sin because God is at the helm of it all. Our sin does not change God's design or desire for his creation. Our sin just makes our job harder.

Now we can see the first two chapters of Genesis in light of God's ultimate purposes: his glory and the flourishing of his creation. In this, our goal is stewardship of all we are and all we have, all the time. This is no light task.

Stewardship comes from the Greek word *oikonomia*, which appears in the New Testament. It is a Greek compound word that is translated as the "management of household affairs, stewardship, and administration."[10] We often think of the word stewardship as synonymous with tithing, church service, or missions. This is a narrow, insufficient understanding of stewardship. In fact, it could lead one to believe the myth that God only cares about the ten percent of your income and four hours per week that you give to the church, nothing else. Not true! God cares about 100 percent of your resources – time, money, skills.

The command in Genesis applies to our whole selves and everything we have. All of our time, creativity, energy, and treasure should be directed to our original job description. We don't get a pass because we misunderstand what God asks of us. The time you spend on the soccer field cheering on your children, reading a novel, or re-painting your bathroom is time God has given you. These things are good if God has called you to them. To be effective stewards we must be wholehearted in our dedication to God's purposes and fulfilling his intent. When we do this with God at the heart of our decisions, we bring him glory and advance his kingdom.

For our hearts to be fully committed to God's purpose, we must have a proper understanding of what God asks of us. God is not asking us to steward *part* of our income, talents, and time. He is asking us to steward *all* of it. The idea of wholeness is vital for stewardship. Wholeheartedness is required. To have God-centered interests we must dedicate our whole selves to his purposes.

Deuteronomy 6:4-5 gives us this command:

> Hear, O Israel: The Lord our God, the Lord is one. Love the Lord your God with all your heart and with all your soul and with all your strength.

This commandment is known as the *Shema,* which means "hear." Theologian Scott Redd writes that wholeness is the goal of redemption in Christ. Redd states that the above verse is not about loving God "a lot"; it is about how our relationship with God should infiltrate every part of our lives.[11] Jesus says that "where your treasure is there your heart will be also," so to be good stewards God must govern our heart, soul, and strength (Matt. 6:21). All of our external choices follow.

Being good stewards, or whole-life stewards, can only come after God changes our hearts and we give our entire person to Christ. Only then can we change what we treasure. All of our choices flow from our desires, so we must continually align our desires with God's desires.

At its core, stewardship is about making choices, and making choices is the science of economics. Making decisions that please God is our goal as God's stewards. Every day, we must choose from many options, and each choice imposes a tradeoff and long-run consequences. Stewardship requires us all to be economists. Even if you were not aware of it, you act as an economist every day. We don't always think of our daily actions as economic choices, but they are. We are called to do these well and with prudence, seeking profit (leftovers) and lowering costs (what we give up). This matters for parents, pastors, and plumbers. No matter who you are or what God has called you to, your job is to do it well. When we think like economists, we are better at counting costs. We have more profit left over with which to serve God's creation. Ultimately, it's his stuff, not ours. He gives us a job that we must do in a way that meets his standards. In doing so, we please and glorify God.

CHAPTER 5:
HOW DO WE MAKE WISE DECISIONS?
Stewardship and the Economic Way of Thinking

Being productive with every choice is difficult. Our sin, our finite knowledge, and our hubris make it difficult. We are constantly the victims of our own sin. This is why it is imperative to understand our origins; understanding how we got here and why we are here is critical for making God-honoring decisions. As we learned in earlier chapters, we have been given all the resources we need to accomplish what God asks of us. Now we must assess the necessary operating environment for success.

Let's turn to Scripture. The parable of the talents is a helpful metaphor for what God asks of us as it relates to fulfilling his desires. It is important to read this text in light of our discussion about God's design and our role as whole-hearted stewards. Matthew 25:14-30 states:

> Again, it will be like a man going on a journey, who called his servants and entrusted his wealth to them. To one he gave five bags of gold, to another two bags, and to another one bag, each according to his ability. Then he went on his journey. The man who had received five bags of gold went at once and put his money to work and gained five bags more. So also, the one with two bags of gold gained two more. But the man who had received one bag went off, dug a hole in the ground and hid his master's money. After a long time the master of those servants returned and settled accounts with them. The man who had received five bags of gold brought the other five. 'Master,' he said, 'you entrusted me with five bags of gold. See, I have gained five more.' His master replied, 'Well done, good and faithful servant! You have been faithful with a few things; I will put you in charge of many things. Come and share your master's happiness!' The man with two bags of gold

also came. 'Master,' he said, 'you entrusted me with two bags of gold; see, I have gained two more.' His master replied, 'Well done, good and faithful servant! You have been faithful with a few things; I will put you in charge of many things. Come and share your master's happiness!' Then the man who had received one bag of gold came. 'Master,' he said, 'I knew that you are a hard man, harvesting where you have not sown and gathering where you have not scattered seed. So I was afraid and went out and hid your gold in the ground. See, here is what belongs to you.' His master replied, 'You wicked, lazy servant! So you knew that I harvest where I have not sown and gather where I have not scattered seed? Well then, you should have put my money on deposit with the bankers, so that when I returned I would have received it back with interest. 'So take the bag of gold from him and give it to the one who has ten bags. For whoever has will be given more, and they will have an abundance. Whoever does not have, even what they have will be taken from them. And throw that worthless servant outside, into the darkness, where there will be weeping and gnashing of teeth.

This passage is about being as productive as we can. The master asked each servant to take what they were given and care for it according to his desires – essentially, to invest his resources in order to make a profit. We are asked to do the same. Profit is about having something left over after one has invested time, talent, and treasure. We think of profit-seeking as relegated to CEOs, and we often think that profit-seekers are evil. This is a misunderstanding of biblical stewardship. Remember Genesis 1. God did not ask Adam and Eve to just watch the Garden of Eden; he told them to work it, to cultivate it, to make it better. We practice good stewardship by carefully, thoughtfully investing God's resources to make the most out of them.

We will know we have stewarded God's creation and our abilities to his glory when we hear the words, "Well done, good and faithful servant! You have been faithful with a few things; I will put you in charge of many things. Come and share your master's happiness!" (Matt. 25:21). We will not just receive praise for our good stewardship, but we will share in the happiness of God. We get closer to shalom in the here and now because we participate in bringing it about. We experience true joy when we do the very best we can with what we have been given. In addition, God rewards good stewardship with more responsibility. There are spiritual and material rewards to good stewardship, both now and eternally.

We can also see from this text that what God gives us is directly related to how he uniquely crafted each of us. No two people are exactly the same. We have different gifts and propensities that are manifested in unique ways. This means that we are all expected to steward in a wholehearted manner but that each of us brings different gifts to the table. Some are "five talent people", some are "one talent people", but we all have talent with expectations.

While we each offer specific gifts, these offerings don't determine our worth. Our worth and dignity come from the one who created us. It is post-modern arrogance to believe that our worth is based on our talents. The truth is we have nothing of value to offer. God bestows our talents upon us and commands us to use them well. We use them well when we profit the most we can.

Note that the master gave each servant at least one talent. We all have gifts and talents to offer; no one can say they do not have any gifts. We have different combinations and different degrees of talents. This parable helps us see that our dignity is not based on how many talents we are given, nor is it based on how much cash is in our bank account. Our dignity comes from our Creator. That you are made in the image of God is what gives you dignity and immense worth. The degree and types of talents that you have will direct how you work, how you serve others, and in what ways. The master gives each servant some of his resources and asks the servant to be productive and create value. We are given the same task. Some of us will net high salaries and some will net smaller salaries. When we are all more productive, even those with small salaries will be rewarded and in a free society will have immense access to goods and services that make life easier and longer.

In expecting us to be productive, God asks us to have leftovers. It is only when we have something left over that we have more to give. Think of it this way: when you save time commuting, you have more time for other things. When you create value at work and receive a bonus, you have more income to invest, spend, or give away. Abundance is a good thing. We should desire leftover time and leftover income so that we can produce more fruit and serve others better. This fruit helps us both physically and spiritually feed others, just as God has designed it.

The costs of not doing this well are tragic. We suffer and become alienated from God, making things harder for both ourselves and others. It is because we are interdependent that the consequences of our actions are not isolated. They have ripple effects on others. The CEO who steals from customers doesn't just harm himself, he harms others and damages the trust in society.

The opposite is also true. The business owner who works with integrity to find better products at cheaper prices serves people, creating positive ripple effects on a society. This does not just occur in the for-profit world of CEOs and customers, as we tend to believe. Matthew 25 reminds us that the master gave different responsibilities to his servants, not necessarily to the most "accomplished" people in society. Whether you are a CEO or the janitor who empties the trash in the CEO's office each day, the pastor or the construction worker who builds the church where the pastor preaches, you are a servant of the master. We do not bring anything to the table on our own. God gives us all our gifts and expects us to use them well, whether in a church or a boardroom.

When we reflect back on the language of Genesis and the word "abad", we are all to serve God and his creation. Each of us is called to service through wholehearted stewardship. Some will be CEOs and some will be janitors. Some will finish college and some will never attend. Some will work as mothers or pastors outside the for-profit realm of modern society, yet all are commanded to seek profit. We all have an essential role to play in God's economy by taking dominion and bearing fruit. When you receive profit, you have served well because you have so prudently used your scarce resources that you have some left over. Leftovers give you additional opportunities to serve.

When the pastor can find a more efficient way to write sermons, he can economize or profit on his time. When a mother can simplify the meal-making process at home, she can profit her time as well. When we have an abundance, whether it's more of our time, money, or energy, we can use it for God's glory. Without profit, we do not have extra to give. Profit is also a signal that we are doing a good job. When we have leftovers, we are accomplishing God's purposes. II Corinthians 5:9 helps us see this:

> So we make it our goal to please him, whether we are at home in
> the body or away from it.

Our goal is always to please God, wherever we are and in whatever we do. We must pursue wholehearted stewardship for the greater flourishing of God's creation. It is as simple and difficult as that. He asks all of us to fulfill this challenge, and we do it through profit-seeking decision-making. This helps us to better steward what God has given us.

CHAPTER 6:
WHAT ARE THE ECONOMIC REALITIES OF STEWARDSHIP?

W
e now have a biblically principled and conceptual understanding of our purpose on earth. In order to fulfill it, we need the proper mechanisms to help us be better stewards. Applying an economic way of thinking to how we make decisions is the best path to achieving wholehearted stewardship of all our time and all our gifts.

ECONOMIC REALITIES

Many Christians disregard economics in making God-honoring decisions because economics seems remote and aggregated. Much of the economics profession has moved toward more aggregation and more sophisticated mathematics over the past century. Some, but not all of that, is a good thing because ultimately, economics starts with people like you and me.

Our new working definition of economics was eloquently explained by economist Ludwig von Mises in 1940 in his seminal work, *Human Action*.[12] Mises defined economics as the science of purposeful human action. In our context, economics is the science of making God-pleasing decisions. If economics is about human action, what drives humans to act? Three things need to be in place for us to act with purpose:

- We must feel some current state of uneasiness that propels us into that action. The presence of sin makes it apparent that the world is not how God intended. Further, God has designed his people with hearts that desire peace and flourishing.

- We need to see a future state where that uneasiness is reduced. The biblical picture of Restoration gives us a vision for what the world one day will be, when all pain, suffering, and tears will be wiped away (Rev. 21:1-4).

- We need to believe that we can get to that future state. As we previously explored, God did not command us to fulfill impossible tasks. He has given his people the necessary tools, gifts, and talents to help bring about flourishing.

Mises, while not a believer, understood the nature of man. He observed the intricacies of God's design for man and creation that we explored in previous chapters. He saw men not as preprogrammed automatons but as individuals with a purpose.

Human Action came about at an important time both in global history and inside the economics profession. The Bolshevik revolution had occurred in 1918 and the Soviet Union was under communist control. Simultaneously, elite academic economists were advocating for central planning, a system where the state owns the means of production and directs economic activity. Central planners had been exercising control for 22 years, and the Soviet empire had not crumbled. It seemed feasible.

Mises saw that even with the best of intentions, central planning disregarded vital elements of human nature (as believers we would call this God's design). Central planning advocates ignored the very elements that Mises understood as critical to human choice. For Mises, to disprove central planning one had to start with the nature of human choice and the realities of humankind.

It is no accident that history proved Mises right, and 49 years after the release of *Human Action*, communism as the world saw it unfold in the Soviet Union failed. Its 71-year reign, which tried to divorce humans from their God-given purpose, in reality killed millions and impoverished more. When we reflect on the language in Genesis and God's creation, we see that this was not his original desire for humankind. The picture in Genesis before the Fall is one of abundance, both spiritually and materially. In contrast, the Soviet Union pitted man against himself by defying man's nature and, in its wake of horror, a godless and poor society worked hard for survival. The Soviet Union provides a profound example of the suffering that occurs when people are hindered from living into their God-designed role. People are limited in their ability to respond to needs, use their gifts to fill voids, and creatively solve problems. When this happens across a society, we see a picture of gray despair–there is no profit. Without anything leftover, we struggle to survive and cannot thrive as much as we should if things worked as God intends them.

Mises developed an economic theory with extraordinary explanatory power because he understood the nature of man. People are purposeful in their actions; they desire something better and take action to remedy their current conditions. From this, we can understand the everyday economic realities that confront us every time we engage in this calculus of choice.

To be effective, wholehearted stewards, we must face five economic realities and incorporate them into our daily decision-making: scarcity, subjective value, self-interest, incentives, and interdependence.

SCARCITY We live in a world of scarcity and we always have, even before the Fall, because we are finite. We have never had infinite knowledge or power. Sin exacerbated the conditions of scarcity by making everything more difficult. Human discovery, entrepreneurship, and learning are all more difficult than they were before sin. We still have to choose, but those choices are less transparent and fraught with our own sinful desires.

The human action model proposed by Mises makes sense only because we must choose, and when we choose, we give up something else. We have unlimited desires but limited means to satisfy those desires. For example, you might have a limited amount of time to eat dinner and exercise. You cannot do both at once, and you might even get sick if you perform them in quick succession. Most of us need to eat with time to digest our food before we exercise and start increasing our heart rate. You have to make a choice. Or, you may want to read a book and prepare dinner. It would save you time if you could do both at once, but because you are finite and limited, you cannot do these things both well and simultaneously. We have to make choices, and when we choose, we face tradeoffs that impose costs. To read the book and understand it, you will have to stop making dinner. Making dinner is the cost to you in this scenario. The cost is always relative for each person and for each decision because we value things differently.

SUBJECTIVE VALUE The idea that we value things differently comes from our uniqueness. We subjectively value things based on our preferences and needs because we are all made with unique gifts and desires. Based on God's intentional design, we value things differently. I may value reading a book more than making a nice dinner. You may value the time it takes to make a beautiful dinner more than reading a book. Subjective value is a characteristic of all people because it is part of how God made us. We have different desires that work their way into what costs we are willing to bear to acquire certain things. If you don't like preparing dinner, you may rely more on frozen food. You prefer frozen food because of the benefit it extends to you (time saved preparing a meal) but that same thing would not be a benefit to another person. Our varied subjective values result in a many options that exist to serve a wide range of different tastes and preferences.

What we value is driven by our unique makeup, personal preferences, and our circumstances at the time. I may choose cake for dessert; you may choose pie. There is no universally "correct" choice here. The world is better when there are more options at a lower cost. Having more options satisfies more preferences, lowers costs, and increases quality. As a result, we all profit more and have leftover resources and time to devote to other pursuits.

SELF INTEREST Subjective value drives our choices or our personal interests and preferences. It simply means that we each value things differently. There is no good or service that has objective value but rather, individuals assign values to things. Each of us assigns values differently based on our preferences. What we view to be in our self-interest is inextricably linked to what we prefer or value. The idea of self-interest can make believers recoil as it is often confused with selfishness. In some way, self-interest is a more benign concept; it is the mechanism of human choice. Recall what Mises asserted: to choose, we need to feel uneasy with our current conditions, we must have a way to improve, and we need a vision for what that improvement looks like. Subjective value determines the "terms" of choice, and we only choose things – out of self-interest – that we prefer over not having them.

When I awake in the morning and make a bowl of oatmeal, I do so in my own self-interest. I am satisfying a need with what I believe will make me better off than I would be if I did not take the action. Of all the foods, I choose oatmeal because I value it over other options to get fueled in the morning. This concept is critical to making God-honoring decisions. I must give my whole heart to God so that I surrender to his will even in eating breakfast. Even these small decisions matter. We may not pray over what to eat for breakfast, but God cares about it because it's a choice that implies a cost. God cares about your breakfast options as much as he cares about who you marry. The breakfast choice is probably an easier one because the cost of a poor choice is small, but whenever we pay a price, we have an opportunity to profit by paying the smallest price possible relative to the potential payoff.

When we dismiss the notion that our lives are all about God and we put ourselves first, our subjective value can become selfish, more focused on what we want, not what God wants. Consequently, things become harder for us. We again become victims of our own sin, and the things we think are good for us actually harm us. Self-interest then involves sacrifice or surrender of my will to God's will. The closer we get to God through prayer and reading his Word, the more we recognize the depth of our sin. Yet, we can still daily seek to surrender our lives to his will with every choice we make.

It is in my own interest to choose Christ and pursue him in every endeavor. I am made to seek profit in all that I do for his purposes so that I can hear "well done good and faithful servant!" and experience joy, fulfillment, and flourishing that I help create. I must have a motivation or reason to do this, so incentives matter.

PROPER INCENTIVES For all of this to work well, we need proper incentives. For the believer, these incentives are pleasing God. God is the originator of incentives. When we seek to please God in all that we do, when we ask him to be present with us in every choice, we can better steward our scarce resources for his glory, and he blesses our efforts. When we act out against God's will and his good design for us, we face frustration; we are pursuing a way the world was not meant to be. Receiving the richness of God's pleasure and blessing based on our obedient stewardship is the ultimate incentive, born out of our response to God's love and grace. Humans will not act without a motive; they must be propelled by their purposes to act. Then when presented with choices we can reason through what is better, although the process of this remains difficult. As the parable of the talents demonstrates, the pleasure of the master is the ultimate incentive.

INTERDEPENDENCE The last fundamental reality is our interdependence. We are made in the image of God but are limited and finite in ways that he is not. We cannot do most things that we need to survive, and this was God's intention. God designed his people to be in community and to rely on each other's gifts and talents. We are finite people who have some gifts, so how is it that we have so many options in our modern world? It is because countries like the United States have implemented systems that allow humans to depend on and serve each other.

Think of all the things you did after you woke up this morning and before you left your house. You may use your smartphone as your alarm clock. You shower using shampoo, conditioner, and soap. You brush your teeth with a toothbrush and toothpaste. You put on clothes that you did not sew. You brew coffee and pour it in a mug. You rinse your empty coffee cup under your faucet of running water and place the mug in the sink. You check your email briefly on your laptop before getting in a car and heading out.

How much of these materials did you make yourself? Most likely, none of them. When we use our gifts, we can focus on the things we are good at doing.

If you are a pastor, utilizing the materials that others have made allows you to prepare a sermon or meet with a member of your church.

Imagine if you had to make your bed from scratch. Most likely, you would be sleeping on the floor or on something that does not resemble your current bed. If you had to make toothpaste, shampoo, ceramic mugs, and laptops, you would never be able to leave the house. You could spend all of your waking hours toiling at things that you were not made to do well and at a very high cost—your time. When you can give up a small portion of your income for ground coffee beans, you don't need to own a farm and roast the beans. Purchasing coffee beans allows you to profit on your time. You can now work on the sermon or go to work as an electrical engineer or a barista.

In order to purchase coffee beans or a bed, we need each other. Our diversity brings us together through trade, allowing us to be interdependent. I go to work and trade my time for income. I can use my income to purchase hotdogs, laptops, and toothpaste. This system of trade is essential for flourishing, and it is only made possible when we can depend on each other. Trading based upon on subjective value allows us to be free to do what God created us to do. We don't have to figure it all out because we were not made to do everything. Only God can do that.

Trade allows us to profit on our time while lowering all of our costs. As we discussed, when we make a choice, we always bear a cost. The cost is the forgone opportunity in that moment in time, known as the opportunity cost. If I spend another hour at night reading my book instead of going to bed, my opportunity cost is an hour of sleep. If I have to make my toothbrush in order to be able to brush and clean my teeth, the opportunity cost is high. It would take all of my waking hours for days and weeks to come up with a far inferior toothbrush compared to what I can purchase at the store for a few dollars. Trade brings strangers together to serve each other. For this to work well, we need a society that embraces the biblical principles of peaceful cooperation.

CHAPTER 7:
WHAT ARE THE REQUIREMENTS FOR FLOURISHING, AND WHAT HAPPENS WITHOUT THEM?

Author James A. Baldwin famously said, "Anyone who has ever struggled with poverty knows how extremely expensive it is to be poor." The poor person has to rely on himself to survive, and survival is often not achieved. The man in the third world who has to hunt for food as his only source of sustenance spends hours doing something that takes just minutes in a grocery store of a wealthy country.

The poor individual pays high opportunity costs to barely meet their most basic needs. In this circumstance, things like floss and toothbrushes seem like inconceivable luxuries. For those that live in societies that reward creating value, people have incentives to serve others. We experience greater flourishing only when we can rely on strangers to provide us with vaccines, medications, and toothbrushes. We profit our time and elongate our lives so that we can do what God created us to do.

To be wholehearted stewards we must not only embrace the economic realities that were outlined in Chapter 5, but we also must be as free as possible to pursue our gifts. We need high levels of freedom to go where God leads us. This was the tragedy of the central planning of the Soviet Union. In a world where dictators rule, the individual serves only to support the state and there is no freedom. The social result is less flourishing and more tragedy and violence. Every time we limit an individual's right to choose and trade, we limit their freedom, and some amount of human flourishing is lost as collateral damage.

To be free in a world where we can love and serve strangers by doing our work well, we need certain institutions: property rights, the rule of law, and prices. We need property rights that are well-defined, well-defended, and transferable. Property rights are the basis of what Peter Boettke called "The Three P's: property right, prices and profits/losses."

PROPERTY RIGHTS

Property rights are a necessary incentive for trade. If I think that after I pay my bill at the grocery store, the owner can take back my cart of food, I won't buy it. My life is worse if I have to forage for food rather than be able to purchase it. Property rights also provide the basis for the emergence of prices. As prices fluctuate, they help us evaluate what we want based on our subjective values. Prices change based on changing scarcity levels and when they do, we re-evaluate each choice, all in the pursuit of profit.

PRICES

Prices also help us seek profit and avoid losses personally and in our business ventures. When someone brings a product to the market, they seek to make money and have residual resources left over. Profits and losses are levied by consumers. The products and services available to us are only available if they are profitable. They are only profitable if they serve the needs of the consumer in some way. Profitable products and services free consumers from figuring out how to do those things on their own. Prices then provide information that we could never acquire on our own. Where prices exist, we are already better off than we would be without them; we have a benchmark to evaluate tradeoffs and economize on our time.

RULE OF LAW

We need the rule of law. The rule of law means that everyone is treated equally before the law, that the law is transparent, laid out in advance, and that the leaders must submit themselves to it. The rule of law prohibits arbitrary behavior on behalf of rulers and allows for predictable behavior on behalf of everyone.

F.A. Hayek, in his famous book *The Road to Serfdom,* warned that as the state plans more of people's lives, we begin to shred the rule of law.[13] As the state takes over more economic activity, we slide into a law of rules rather than the rule of law. Leaders will start to change the rules to suit their will rather than submit their arbitrary whims of power to a pre-existing set of rules. This happens precisely because the state does not have any idea how to order economic affairs. They don't know whether you like almond butter or peanut butter, crunchy or smooth, organic or not. Not only do they not know, but they do not have the incentives to learn your preferences for peanut butter. Makers of peanut butter do have incentives, because you reward them by giving them money for whatever flavor you choose. They have incentives to make their products better, cheaper, and safer over time because they are competing to serve you.

Without the rule of law, we lose predictability of state behavior. I am confident that state agents will not break into my house and steal all my possessions because they are also subject to the rule of law. The rule of law limits the state's ability to plunder and to infringe on our ability to choose as God directs us. When we live in a society with the rule of law, we can make plans for the future, for living out God's desires in our life. If God is calling you to open a business or a church, property rights and rule of law will make that much easier. You can raise money for investments in buildings and businesses. The rule of law is essential for well-protected, well-defined, and transferable property rights.

When we have property rights and the rule of law combined with political, religious, and economic freedom, we can pursue God's purposes as they pertain to our unique lives. When any of these three freedoms are limited, we are less free to be wholehearted stewards.

ECONOMIC FREEDOM

Economic freedom, or freedom to make economic exchanges as one sees fit, is critical to our pursuits. The more economic freedom we have to make choices as God directs us, the more societal flourishing we both contribute to and experience. God says to the faithful servant that he will experience the happiness of his master. When we have greater societal flourishing, the costs we face when we make choices decrease, and it is mechanically easier to serve God. Our hearts always need to be redirected towards his will, but greater material flourishing makes it easier to profit our time that we can redirect to God.

We measure economic freedom using *The Economic Freedom of the World*, an annual survey that measures the extent to which individuals in a society are free to make economic choices, such as what they want to buy and sell, and whether they can easily start a business.[14] When societies are governed by economic systems that embrace God's design for creation, people experience much greater levels of human flourishing. When societies do not allow individuals to make choices over their own lives as God is leading them, there is great suffering.

Countries such as the United States, which for many years was a leader in economic freedom metrics, experienced great life-saving and life-extending innovations. In these societies, the material benefits of these innovations extend across income groups and destroy more primitive cultures of political classicism based on birthright. Societies that score well on the economic freedom index allow individuals from all walks of life – rich and poor, old and young, highly educated or not – to have a chance to use their creativity to serve others.

My experience in the Soviet Union demonstrated to me what life looks like without economic freedom. The words of Thomas Hobbes were a reality:

> No arts; no letters; no society; and which is worst of all, continual
> fear, and danger of violent death: and the life of man, solitary,
> poor, nasty, brutish and short.[15]

Everyone lived in a real fear of violent death, if not a quick death by the gas chamber, then a slow death by starvation. Life was nasty and short and miserable because society did not respect our God-given design. Stalin and Lenin were not historical anomalies; they were the direct result of a society that tried to plan all economic life. Totalitarian oppression is the modus operandi in a life without the necessary freedom for us to make God-pleasing decisions in our own lives.

I want to end with a famous story which I first read in Thomas Sowell's book *Basic Economics* that illustrates the stark difference in societies that embrace economic freedom and those that try to stamp it out.[16] It is a true story of Boris Yelstin, who came to the United States in September of 1989. Yeltsin was newly elected to the Soviet Parliament and the Supreme Soviet. At this time, the economic collapse of the Soviet Union was looming but had not yet happened. Yeltsin and his cronies were visiting the Johnson Space Center in Texas. After they left, they made an unscheduled trip to Randall's Grocery Store in Houston, Texas.

That grocery store experience changed Yeltsin forever, and he went on to write about it later in his autobiography. He roamed the aisles to see products in wide variety waiting for customers. The store was offering free cheese samples. Yeltsin was overwhelmed. He could not believe the bounty before him, and that there was no fanfare about it; it was just an ordinary day.[17] Yeltsin said that even the elite Politburo did not have these choices, and he asked the store manager if he required a special education to manage a store like Randall's.

Yeltsin was a powerful, elite, and politically connected man. He was more powerful than most of us will ever be in political terms, yet economically he was powerless. Despite his intellect and numerous connections, he could not make grocery stores happen in the Soviet Union. The house was built on sand. There were no property rights, no incentives to create, and no freedom.

One year after Yeltsin's experience in Houston, he would talk about it despondently:

> When I saw those shelves crammed with hundreds, thousands of cans, cartons and goods of every possible sort, for the first time I felt quite frankly sick with despair for the Soviet people," Yeltsin wrote. "That such a potentially super-rich country as ours has been brought to a state of such poverty! It is terrible to think of it."[18]

It is terrible to think about because it is not the way it is supposed to be. The Soviet episode occurred because leaders wanted their own power at the expense of humanity.

When we are relatively freer to be who God created us to be, we advance his kingdom both today and eternally. Nothing we do is wasted if we pursue it with integrity, honesty, prudence, and a wholehearted dedication to God. It all matters, and we are called to do it all well.

This booklet began with a story about my experience in the former Soviet Union. When we take God out of our decisions, we become deluded with power and the desire to hurt others to accomplish our selfish goals. The Soviet Union was an economy-wide effort in doing this. The only predictable things over the 71 years of that reign were suffering, violence, and terror. People starved at the hands of the state. We must be free in every aspect to live as God intends in order to experience the greater flourishing that glorifies God. When we do this, we build up his creation rather than destroy it. God tasks us with caring for and cultivating his good creation until the day he returns or calls us home. What an honor to be part of God's perfect work. We should start renewed with the task of using the realities of economics to allow us and others to practice what God commands: wholehearted stewardship.

ENDNOTES

1. Courtois, Stéphane, and Mark Kramer, eds. *The Black Book of Communism: Crimes, Terror, Repression*. Cambridge, MA: Harvard University Press, 1999.

2. Grudem, Wayne A. *Systematic Theology: An Introduction to Biblical Doctrine*. Grand Rapids: Zondervan, 1994.

3. Staub, Dick. "What Made in the Image of God Really Means." Relevant. March 4, 2013. http://www.relevantmagazine.com/god/deeper-walk/features/23549-qmade-in-the-image-of-godq.

4. Staub, Dick. "What Made in the Image of God Really Means." Relevant. March 4, 2013. http://www.relevantmagazine.com/god/deeper-walk/features/23549-qmade-in-the-image-of-godq.

5. "Strong's Hebrew: 5647. עָבַד (abad) — to Work, Serve." Strong's Hebrew: 5647. עָבַד (abad) — to Work, Serve. http://biblehub.com/hebrew/5647.htm.

6. Pennington, Jonathan. "A Biblical Theology of Human Flourishing." The Institute for Faith, Work & Economics. http://tifwe.org/resources/a-biblical-theology-of-human-flourishing-2/.

7. Plantinga, Cornelius. *Not the Way It's Supposed to Be: A Breviary of Sin*. Grand Rapids, MI: Eerdmans, 1995.

8. Keller, Timothy. *Generous Justice: How God's Grace Makes Us Just*. New York, NY: Dutton, Penguin Group USA, 2010.

9. Whelchel, Hugh. *How Then Should We Work?: Rediscovering the Biblical Doctrine of Work*. Bloomington, IN: West Bow Press, 2012.

10. "Strong's Greek: 3622. οἰκονομία (oikonomia) — Stewardship, Administration." Strong's Greek: 3622. οἰκονομία (oikonomia) — Stewardship, Administration. http://biblehub.com/greek/3622.htm.

11. Redd, Scott. *Wholehearted: A Biblical Look at the Greatest Commandment and Personal Wealth*. McLean: The Institute for Faith, Work & Economics, 2016.

12. Mises, Ludwig Von. *Human Action: A Treatise on Economics*. Auburn Ala.: Ludwig Von Mises Institute, 2008.

13. Hayek, Friedrich A. Von, and Bruce Caldwell. *The Road to Serfdom: Text and Documents*. Chicago: University of Chicago Press, 2007.

14. Gwartney, James, Robert Lawson, and Joshua Hall. *2015 Economic Freedom Dataset*. Report. Frasier Institute, 2015. http://www.freetheworld.com/datasets_efw.html.

15. Hobbes, Thomas, and Richard Tuck. *Leviathan*. Cambridge: Cambridge University Press, 1991.

16. Sowell, Thomas. *Basic Economics: A Common Sense Guide to the Economy*. New York: Basic Books, 2007.

17. Hlavaty, Craig. "When Boris Yeltsin Went Grocery Shopping in Clear Lake." The Houston Chronicle. April 7, 2014. http://blog.chron.com/thetexican/2014/04/when-boris-yeltsin-went-grocery-shopping-in-clear-lake/.

18. Ibid.

ABOUT THE AUTHOR
ANNE RATHBONE BRADLEY, PHD

D r. Anne Rathbone Bradley is the vice president of economic initiatives at the institute, where she develops and commissions research toward a systematic biblical theology of economic freedom.

She is a visiting professor at Georgetown University, and she also teaches at the Institute for World Politics and George Mason University. Additionally, she is a visiting scholar at the Bernard Center for Women, Politics, and Public Policy. Previously, she taught at Charles University, Prague, and served as the associate director for the Program in Economics, Politics, and the Law at the James M. Buchanan Center at George Mason University.

She is an editor of and contributing author to IFWE's recently released book, *For the Least of These: A Biblical Answer to Poverty.* In her chapter, Dr. Rathbone Bradley examines income inequality from both an economic and biblical perspective and provides guidance to Christians on how to respond, particularly through our vocations.

Dr. Rathbone Bradley's other academic work has focused on the political economy of terrorism with specific emphasis on the industrial organization of al-Qaeda. Her research has been published in scholarly journals and edited volumes. She is currently working on a book that analyzes the political economy of al-Qaeda post–9/11. Based on her academic research, she also worked as an economic analyst for the Central Intelligence Agency's Office of Terrorism Analysis.

Dr. Rathbone Bradley received her PhD in economics from George Mason University in 2006, during which time she was a James M. Buchanan Scholar. ∎

ABOUT THE INSTITUTE
FOR FAITH, WORK & ECONOMICS

The Institute for Faith, Work & Economics™ (IFWE) is a nonprofit, 501(c)(3) Christian research organization committed to promoting biblical and economic principles that help individuals find fulfillment in their work and contribute to a free and flourishing society.

IFWE's research starts with the belief that the Bible, as the inerrant Word of God, provides the authoritative and intellectual foundation for a proper understanding of work and economic truths that, when properly followed, can help individuals, companies, communities, and nations flourish.

IFWE's research is based on three core principles:

- Each person is created in God's image and, like him, has a desire to be creative and to find **fulfillment** using their God-given talents through work.
- All work, whether paid or volunteer, matters to God, and we as Christians are called to pursue excellence throughout the week—not just on Sundays—stewarding all that we've been given for God's glory and for the **flourishing** of society.
- Therefore, we as citizens must promote an economic environment that not only provides us the **freedom** to pursue our callings and flourish in our work but also reflects the inherent dignity of every human being.

Our desire is to help Christians view their work within the bigger picture of what God is doing in the world. Not only do we help Christians find personal fulfillment, but we also help them understand how to better alleviate poverty, address greed, and view possessions properly. With a biblical view of work and economics, we can partner together to be meaningful participants in God's plan to restore the world to the way he intended it to be.

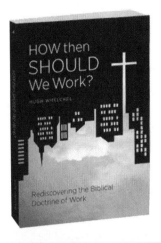
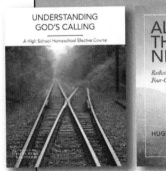

START HERE

The Institute for Faith, Work & Economics provides many resources to help you live a life of freedom, fulfillment, and flourishing. These tools are designed to fit into your life and provide biblical encouragement and guidance to your walk with God.

BLOG
Get our daily or weekly blog updates in your inbox.
BLOG.TIFWE.ORG

RESEARCH
Download free in-depth studies to further your understanding of faith, work, and economics.
RESEARCH.TIFWE.ORG

SOCIALIZE
Connect with IFWE on social media and join the conversation.
FACEBOOK.COM / FAITHWORKECON
TWITTER.COM / FAITHWORKECON

BOOK STORE

Get our latest releases and
educational products.

STORE.TIFWE.ORG

DONATE

Become a partner in bringing
about flourishing.

DONATE.TIFWE.ORG

PARTICIPATE

Find information about student
groups, upcoming events, and other
opportunities to get involved.

CONNECT.TIFWE.ORG

INSTITUTE FOR
FAITH, WORK
& ECONOMICS

INSTITUTE FOR
FAITH, WORK
& ECONOMICS

Made in the USA
Charleston, SC
03 March 2017